SINAI
AND THE RED SEA

Text by
Giovanna Magi

BONECHI

© Copyright by CASA EDITRICE BONECHI
Via Cairoli 18b - 50131 Firenze - Italia
Fax +39 0555000766
E-mail: bonechi@bonechi.it - Internet: www.bonechi.it

Project and editorial conception: Casa Editrice Bonechi
Publication Manager: Serena de Leonardis
Picture research: Serena de Leonardis
Cover: Sonia Gottardo
Text: Giovanna Magi

Printed in Italy by Centro Stampa Editoriale Bonechi - Sesto Fiorentino

Photographs from the archives of Casa Editrice Bonechi *taken by* Serena de Leonardis, Marco Eletti, A. Fantauzzo, Paolo Giambone, A. Innocenti, Stefano Landini *and* Red Sea Marine.

Pages 15 above, 16, 22 right, 23, 24 below left, 25 above right, 27 above right, 29, 33: Ghigo Roli; *pages 91/121:* Andrea Ghisotti.

ISBN 88-476-0938-0

* * *

Meeting a tribe of Bedouins is quite a frequent occurrence in the desert.

THE SINAI PENINSULA

GEOGRAPHY

"A thousand square kilometers of nothing" is the description often given to the Sinai peninsula. In fact, at first glance, Sinai seems to be a boundless moon landscape, arid and barren in its immense mountains, in its parched "ouadi", in its stony stretches that have never known either man's labours or the presence of animals.

Aside from the few tribes of Bedouins, who have by now replaced the roomy black tents made of canvas with much more prosaic shelters of corrugated sheet iron, the desert belongs today — just as it did three thousand years ago — to the fox and the wolf, to the gazelle and to the wild goat.

The name "Sinai" can perhaps be connected to Sin, the goddess of the moon, who was adored by the ancient inhabitants of the desert, or maybe to the Semitic word "sen" which means tooth.

About twenty million years ago, Egypt, Sinai and the Arab peninsula were united in a single block. Then, huge terrestrial devastations led to the separation of the lands, and the southern Sinai peninsula remained isolated, giving rise to two large gulfs: to the west, the Gulf of Suez, whose maximum depth is barely 95 metres, and the Gulf of Aqaba to the east, which instead reaches a depth of 1,800 metres. The latter gulf is a part of the big land fissure — called Rift — which extends from the chain of Taurus as far as Kenya. The great sismic activity of the past and the tremendous eruptive phenomena have given Sinai its characteristic imprint. The mountains there range from 750 to 2500 metres; the most important peaks are the Gebel Musa (Moses' mountain), that reaches 2285 metres, and Mount St Catherine (Gebel Kathrina), of 2642 metres, the highest on the peninsula.

It can be said that all of southern Sinai is like a wild scenario in which the different rock strata, with their different colour gradations, narrate the thousands of years of history of this land of barren beauty.

Minerals are represented there a little bit everywhere: from limestone in its ochre and white varieties to loam rocks, whose wide brown strata alternate with the greenish stripes of the feldspars; from azurite, with its beautiful blue colour, to granite, present in all its grey, pink and yellow varieties. Only 60 millimetres of rain fall annually on southern Sinai, giving rise to the thick vegetation which is found in numerous "ouadi". In winter, the precipitations are often so copious that they rapidly fill the natural wells and give rise to very green oases abounding in palm trees and tamarisks. The west coast, then, that from Sharm el Sheikh to Ras Mohammed goes as far as Taba, is distinguished by numerous coral reefs that occur in succession, one after the other, creating the ideal conditions for a flora and a marine fauna, the variety and richness of which have no peer in other seas.

HISTORY

"And they took their journey from Elim, and all the congregation of the children of Israel came unto the wilderness of Sin, which is between Elim and Sinai, on the fifteenth day of the second month after their departing out of the land of Egypt" (Exodus, 16:1).

Thus, Sinai entered the history of mankind with a very precise date. Despite the controversies among historians, scientists and archaeologists, Sinai has always been associated with the biblical exodus, with the wanderings of the children of Israel, with the Tables of the Law that God dictated to Moses. Sinai has not only been the dramatic stage for a biblical event: it has been the setting for one of the most important human events — that in which a man who was born and grew up in a polytheistic historical context, gave to the people the laws of a single God. It mattered little whether the path of the children of Israel went more to the north or more to the south; it was of little importance whether the exact location of the mount which Moses ascended is still the subject of controversies between scientists. The fact remains that in this solitary, wild land took place one of the events which have created history.

The importance, not just religious, of these places is also marked by the fact that through them passed the armies of numerous powers, from those of the Egyptians Tutmosis III and Ramsete II to those of the Persian Cambises; from those of Greeks Alexander the Great to those of the Romans of Antioch. And then again, the Arabs and the Crusades, Napoleon and Lawrence, up until the last, most recent ones of Israel and Egypt.

Here on Sinai runs the road travelled by the thousands of Egyptian slaves who worked in the copper and turquoise mines; there also winds the road pounded by the thousands of pilgrims, Christian and ascetes who, when the persecutions became more stringent, sought a refuge here for their salvation and a consolation to their prayers, in spite of the dangers and privations which they had constantly had to undergo from hostile tribes and from the unfriendly nature that surrounded them.

According to the tradition subsequently perpetuated by a whole series of travellers, on Sinai celebrated episodes took place that were connected with Moses, from that of the burning bush to that of the manna falling from heaven; but the main one was that of the Tables of the Law which God gave to the children of Israel.

A study of nature as found on Sinai has furnished a scientific explanation for the first two of these "traditions".

"And he looked and behold, the bush burned with fire, and the bush was not consumed" (Exodus, 3:2). There actually exist two hypotheses for explaining this phenomenon. The first is based on the existence of a gaseous plant called *Dictamnus albus*, having many pods full of an extremely fluid oil which catches on fire in the presence of a flame. The second hypothesis depends on the presence in this zone of the *Loranthus acaciae*, a branch of *mistletoe* with crimson flowers. When the moment of full bloom is reached, it takes on the appearance of a bush in flames.

As to the second episode, that of the "bread from heaven", the Bedouins still today gather the Mann-es-Samâ in the early morning. Sweet as honey, it has the look and size of a seed of coriander. It grows on the *Tamarix Mannifera*, a species of accacia that is very diffuse in this zone.

With regard to the third episode, the most well-known one, the Bible tells how God revealed Himself to Moses on Mount Sinai: *"[...] For they [...] were come to the desert of Sinai, and had pitched in the wilderness; and there Israel camped before the Mount. And Moses went up into God [...]"* (Exodus, 19: 2,3). *"So Moses went down unto the people, and spake unto them. And God spake all these words, saying, I am the Lord thy God [...] Thou shalt have no other gods before me"* (Exodus 19:25; 20:1,2,3).

One of the two summits, the Gebel Musa and the Ras-es-Safsafeh which are located in this zone, is today identified with the Mount of the Wooden Tablets.

A series of painstaking scientific explorations has made it possible today to throw light upon the difficult march of the Hebrews through the desert, the march of a huge community of men and beasts which lasted a good forty years, ever searching for a well of water or for a verdant oasis.

It is not known exactly how many people left Egypt in that month of April during the reign of Ramsete II: certainly, it is not thinkable that there were the three million as mentioned in the book of Exodus! Much more realistically, the archaeologist Flinders Petrie calculates the number to have been about 27,000.

There exist three current theories on the presumed path taken by Moses from Egypt to the promised land of Canaan. The first is the traditional one: i.e. the Israelites reached the Red Sea by passing close to Suez and crossing it near Ain Musa. The second theory is that the march took place more to the south, and that the crossing of the waters occurred at Ain Sukhna.

On the preceding page, the rocky desert and the mountains of the Sinai peninsula.

Three aerial views of the unmistakable landscape of the Red Sea.

The third theory is that the march took place more to the north, on the Nile Delta in the direction of the Salt Lakes. Today this third theory is the most accredited one. Various factors stand in its favour, the first one among which is that only to the north are there enough pastures, vegetation and oases to have given food and drink to that large a number of people and animals over a period of forty years. Even the tamarisk trees which produce manna are much more numerous to the north than to the south.

In the second place, they had marched south, the Hebrews would have found along their route the numerous garrisons of Egyptian soldiers which Ram-

sete II had set up in order to guard the copper and turquoise mines that he had reactivated on Sinai: this was a danger which the Hebrews would certainly have wanted to avoid.

In any case, whichever itinerary was the one followed by Moses and by his multitude of Hebrews, it is certain that the localities of Sinai — thanks also to the presence of the monastery of St Catherine — continue to attract, today just as they did many centuries ago, pilgrims and worshippers, travellers and tourists, who follow these paths of faith and tradition that were traced in times past by all those who visited or lived in these places.

Two views of Na'ama Bay, a few kilometers from Sharm el Sheikh, today a primary tourist resort with excellent structures and services.

SHARM EL SHEIKH

Sharm el Sheikh is one of the greatest tourist successes in recent years: the exceptional strategic importance of its location, at the confluence of the Gulfs of Suez and Aqaba, enabled the Israeli soldiers during the Six-Day War to advance this far, setting under way that development of the village which continues still today. When the Camp David agreements gave Sinai back to Egypt, the trenches and bunkers were destroyed and the military buildings were modified so as to be suitable as tourist residences.

Sharm el Sheikh definitely has a charm of its own: risen practically out of nothing, it is squeezed between the rocky mass of Sinai behind and the incredible blue of the Red Sea in front. All around are sandy dunes, the rare oasis, camels and tents belonging to the Bedouins. In just a few years, first-class hotel complexes have sprung up, boasting all the equipment and comforts necessary for ensuring for the tourist a prolonged and enjoyable stay.

Here at Sharm el Sheikh, it is impossible for a tourist to be bored: from diving, where a simple mask is enough to be able to admire the fish gliding tranquilly by in a fantasy world, in no way frightened by the presence of human beings, to rides on horses and

The splendid Na'ama Bay with its modern hotel complexes and beach.

A panoramic view of Sharm el Sheikh against the backdrop of the mountains of the Sinai.

camels; from outings among the rocks of Sinai, where breathtaking views carry us back to biblical times, to boat rides; from walks along the sandy coast to hours spent lazily getting a suntan or having a look around the shops which sell typical artisan products and Egyptian and Bedouin clothing.

The evening at Sharm el Sheikh, then, is magic time: all the lights in the village go on, the streets come alive, the tables outside the bars and restaurants fill up with people.

They smoke the narghile, drink Turkish coffee, savour the long night of Sharm el Sheikh, as a new day is awaited that will bring, as usual, many new opportunities for amusement and relaxation.

11

On these pages: some views of the beach and the sea at Sharm el Sheikh.

The beach for the Sharm el Sheikh hotels, with their typical beach umbrellas, palm trees and luxuriant oleanders.

Na'ama Bay , the tourist center of Sharm el Sheikh, is studded with hotel complexes with avant-garde facilities.
In the photograph, the pools of the Novotel, the Galy Land, and the Hotel Hilton Fayrouz.

At Sharm el Sheikh, every hotel has its own well-equipped beach.

Every day, numerous boats carry off skin-diving enthusiasts to discover the wonders and secrets of the depths of the Red Sea.

The Golf Hotel and its playing fields, at Sharm el Sheikh.

The clear waters of the sea at Sharm el Sheikh and the beach with its facilities for vacationers.

Views of the Sharm el Sheikh Bay with its
marvelous waters.

At Sharm el Sheikh, it is as easy to rent a bicycle as it is to purchase local handcrafts products.

The images on these pages convey the cordial atmosphere of the streets of Sharm el Sheikh, with its shops, restaurants, and craftsmen at work.

Near Sharm el Sheikh is Shark Bay, a true aquatic paradise.

SHARK BAY

Notwithstanding the aggressive and perilous name —
bay of sharks — it is difficult to imagine a place so rich
in peace and tranquil beauty as this is.

Here the sea comes to lap gently against the stony
beach of this small bay protected by rocky dunes: the
reef begins here, at a few swimming strokes from the
shore, and it is immediately an immersion in an unreal,
imaginative world populated by creatures which seem
born more of the fantasy of an abstract or psychodael-
ic painting than of a severe and exacting nature.

It seems that man has always been afraid to touch this
corner of paradise: no gaudy buildings, but only Bedouin tents covered with an unobtrusive pergola; only
the affability and cordiality of the inhabitants of the
village, who offer their proverbial and exquisite hospi-
tality to visitors with a smile.

The beach and the coastline of El Fanar.
The beauties of the reef are clearly visible
in its crystalline waters.

The road leading to the Ras Mohammed National Park is marked by curious pyramidal structures and arches of artificial stone.

An aerial view of the Ras Mohammed coastline with its coral sea bottom.

RAS MOHAMMED NATIONAL PARK

For the joy of those who love uncontaminated and uncorrupted nature, for all those people who search for wealth and variety in flora and marine fauna, Ras Mohammed National Park, at a few kilometers from Sharm el Sheikh, is without doubt an ideal spot.

Declared a protected area in 1983, the park is flanked to the east by the Gulf of Aqaba and to the west by the Gulf of Suez. A series of obligatory paths, marked by different colours, cross the park so that the visitor can go and discover the most charming spot, the most hidden little inlet, the most isolated beach, the most curious and special scenic shortcut.

There can be found a large number of different animals, from the desert fox to the hyena, from the gazelle to the ibis and, among the birds, the Pandion haliaetus, or osprey, two types of storks, the white and the black, and the elegant ash-grey heron.

Due to the very particular conditions of the water, that is transparent and with temperatures of +20 degrees, at Ras Mohammed there is one of the most beautiful coral reefs in the world. There, the reef contains more than 150 different species of corals; in addition, there can be found examples of all of the other thousand species of fish that live in the Red Sea. To list them, even in minimal part, is impossible; but we can certainly not forget the bright apple-green *Cheilins undulatus*, or the *Thalassoma purpureum*, whose turquoise body is furrowed with reddish streaks, or the *Chaetodon semilarvatus*, with a black eye in a completely orange body, or yet again the royal angel shark, or the *Pygoplites diacanthus* with its yellow-blue stripes.

31

Ancient coral formations crop out in the sandy beach.

*Facing page, Ras Mohammed National Park.
The aerial roots of the mangroves (Avicennia marina)
and the natural arch of Yolanda Bay.*

And how can we fail to be fascinated by the perilous beauty of the stone fish, the famous *Synacea verrucosa*, which camouflages itself with the sandy depths until it completely disappears.

As far as the flora is concerned, for all that it is extremely sparse, at Ras Mohammed there can be found magnificent examples of Mangrove: those in the Park are the plants which grow more to the north of the Indian Ocean. The Mangrove, which belongs to the family of the Rhizophoraceae, constitutes an important ecosystem for the coastal zones with a tropical climate. They grow in saline and lagoonal zones; they have pneumatophore: that is, respiratory roots, which protrude from the mud and from the water, ensuring the exchange of oxygen.

The Rock World

Whoever today ventures along the paths that cross the area of the Sinai peninsula is certain of enjoying one of the most magnificent and moving sights that Nature can offer.

Fortunately, during its long, anguished and tormented history, this land has remained uncorrupted. Today it is Nature, not man, who is the sole master; yet, at the same time, it bears testimony to the passing of time that has not changed at all over the centuries.

Entering the magic world of Sinai is to enter the world of its rugged rocks, in the unforeseeable scenario of the sand dunes — ready to change form the moment the desert wind changes its direction. It means penetra-ting the secret of Bedouin life, with its unchanged antique existence, scanned by the same things and the same habits of three thousand years ago. It signifies adventuring into the dried-up bed of an "ouadi", where everything seems to be rock and only rock, and to suddenly discover a vegetation which perseveres in living and in growing.

Over and above the spirituality that the tourist can find within the walls of the monastery of St. Catherine, this all emanates from Sinai, from this world of rock and sand, of solitude and silence.

This is perhaps one of the few places in the world in which man can hope to find himself again.

Rocks and sandy dunes alternate in the typical Sinai landscape.

On the following pages, views of the rocky Sinai Desert, the Bedouins who inhabit it, and their tents and homes.

The dazzling colours of the dress of a Bedouin woman: the essential accessory has always been and still is today the veil. Women do not willingly accept to have their picture taken, and as soon as they catch sight of the indiscreet lens of a camera, they rapidly pull down over their faces the mantle that they wear resting on their heads.

The simple but highly coloured tunics of three Bedouin girls stand out against the desert sand.

Two Bedouins with their camels in the desert in the direction of St Catherine.

On these pages and the following pages: along the road leading to St Catherine are found these strange rocky forms caused by the wind's erosion. Again, three corroded, smooth rocks, sculpted by the desert wind.

Two views of the Monastery of St Catherine, in the heart of the Sinai. Seen from a plane, the monastery looks almost like a child's toy abandoned in the immense rocky desert.

MONASTERY OF ST CATHERINE

HISTORY

The smallest diocesis in the world is at the same time the oldest Christian monastery still in existence in the world and houses also the richest collection of icons and precious manuscripts.

We can find the first news regarding the Monastery of St Catherine in the chronicles of the Patriarch of Alexandria, Entychios, who lived during the 9th century: said chronicles tell us how Helena, the mother of Emperor Constantine, remained so impressed by the sacredness of these places that in the year 330 she ordered the construction of a small chapel on the site where the burning bush had been located. The chapel was dedicated to the Blessed Virgin Mary.

During the years that followed, if on the one hand the ever-growing attention of Christianity in the monastery brought about its enrichment through ever more numerous ecclesiastic donations, on the other hand it led to a series of raids and murders, carried out, by the nomadic tribes of the desert.

These bloody raids against the monks and hermits went on for the entire 6th century, until Emperor Justinian in 530 ordered the construction of a much larger basilica: the one which would be the Church of the Transfiguration. It was then that the monastery took on the appearance of a massive fortification which characterizes it even today. In order to protect the monks from possible incursions, in fact, Justinian had a genuine fort constructed around the church. In 640, after the Arab conquest of Egypt, the monastery became an out- of-the-way bulwark of Christianity in the boundless world of Islam. According to tradition, Mohammed in person granted his protection to a delegation of monks who had gone to see the Prophet. A copy of the document attesting to this protection can still be seen today in the monastery.

In 726 iconoclasm began, and Emperor Leo III ordered the destruction of all the images in the Christian communities: in its magnificent isolation, the monastery of St Catherine was the only one to succeed in maintaining intact its enormous, valuable artistic

Three views of the powerful enclosing walls that surround the monastery, with the round towers that lighten and mitigate the severity of the building.

patrimony. Peace and stability continued to reign in the monastery even during the troubled period of the Crusades.

The war for the liberation of the Holy Places brought important personages, such as Henry II of Brunswick, Philip of Artois and Duke Albert of Austria, to visit the monastery.

For all the centuries that followed, the monastery witnessed the arrival of travellers who, attracted by the charm of the biblical localities, faced numerous dangers and not-indifferent discomforts in order to visit this land: the more daring ones ventured to climb the holy mountains. These first tourists came from almost all the European countries: they were English, French, German and Dutch, and they willingly left their names scribbled as graffiti on the walls of the buildings, particularly on those of the refectory.

During Napoleon's short-lived adventure in Egypt, the scholars who followed the Napoleonic army and described Sinai and the monastery were mostly French. This subsequently led to an ever-growing number of travellers, above all painters and writers. The 19th century brought with it, among other things, also a new concept of travel, and tourism in the

modern sense began to be spoken of: whoever went to visit the Holy Land could not help but include an excursion to Mount Sinai and to the monastery of St Catherine in their itinerary.

The touristic development of these zones kept on increasing in time. Nowadays, the construction of convenient asphalted roads, the building of well-equipped hotel complexes and, lastly, also the birth of a small airport in the environs, have meant that ever more numerous groups of tourists choose this remote place, not yet touched by the modern world, as their travel destination.

Still today, the monastery belongs to the Greek Orthodox Church, and most of the monks who live there are Greek: there, they practice the rules of the order of St Basil the Great, who was Bishop of Cesarea and who lived between 329 and 379.

The Abbot of the monastery is elected by the four Archimandrites, and is consacrated by the Patriarch of Jerusalem, who is one of the six ecumenical Greek-Orthodox patriarchs, together with those of Rome, Moscow, Alexandria, Constantinople and Antioch. As Archbishop of Sinai, the Abbot wears the mitre and the crown, and carries the sceptre and the gold cross.

Outside

Located at an altitude of 1570 metres, at the end of a narrow valley, made even tinier by the high mountains that loom up there, the monastery of St Catherine immediately appears before us in all of its imposing fortified structure, with the walls of local red granite which surround it. The area around it is roughly an irregular quadrangle of approximately 85 x 74 metres. The height of the walls varies from 12 to 15 metres, and the thickness is as much as 1.65 metres. Along its path there are numerous Maltese crosses going back to the 6th century. At each corner, facing in the direction of a cardinal point, rises a tower, while a communication trench for the guard runs along the inside; the east corner is protected by the so-called "Kleber tower".

On the wall to the northwest can still be seen today the ancient windlass which made entry to the monastery and the supply of food possible, both for the monks and for the pilgrims who stopped at the foot of the walls. Directly under this "lift" is located the door by which visitors today can enter the monastery: the original entry door, on the right, was closed during the

Middle Ages by way of defense, thus leaving on the ground floor no other access to the monastery.

Inside

Upon entering the inside of the monastery, one's first impression is that of entering a medieval village: the buildings are crowded together, each one of a different shape, style and size. Small courtyards, staircases, galleries surrounding the buildings, narrow corridors, vaulted arcades and rounded arches, pointed roofs and flat roofs, the bell tower and the minaret of the mosque: everything seems to have sprung up by chance, without any order or precise criterion.

And yet the sense of harmony and of spirituality that emanates from it is great.

In addition to the Basilica of the Transfiguration, there are also twenty chapels in the monastery: they are dedicated to the Blessed Virgin Mary and to the Patron Saints, and are only used for celebrating the relative feast days. Various wells provide water for the monastery. The most important one, located on the

The copy of the document with which the prophet Mohammed guaranteed protection to the monastery.

The windlass with which the ancient entry door to the monastery was operated.

A view of the inside of the monastery complex.

right after the entrance, is the well known as Bir Musa, or **Moses' well**. Tradition has it that it was here that Moses met Jethro's daughters, the oldest of whom, Zipporah, subsequently became his wife.

BASILICA OF THE TRANSFIGURATION

More than a basilica, this is a genuine museum, thanks to the quantity and great value of the works contained in it.

Entrance to the basilica is through a massive 12th-century entry door, in the Fatimid style: this door opens directly onto the narthex where, under thick protective glass, is displayed a marvellous collection of icons dating from the 5th to 7th centuries. Recalling all of them is impossible, but the most memorable ones are those of *St Peter and the Virgin with Child between St Theodore and St George*, that of the *Ascension of Christ*, that of *Christ the Pantocrator*, etc.

Let us go beyond yet another door, this too magnificent: it is believed to be the original one of the church of Justinian, and it is one of the very rare wooden

The Basilica of the Transfiguration: a detail of the façade with the bell tower.

A fresco in a lunette depicting the Transfiguration of Christ.

doors of the early Christian centuries that have come down to us. It is formed of twenty-eight panels inlayed with typically Christian motifs, such as the peacock, the vine, etc.

The inside, 40 metres long and 20 metres wide, has three naves divided by twelve monolithic granite columns, each one representing the twelve months of the year, and is decorated with the icon of the saint venerated during the month in question. Each column is surmounted by a massive capital decorated with historical scenes, each different from the other. The central nave ends with the apse; the lateral naves, with two chapels. The richly-inlaid seats that are set between the columns are exceptionally beautiful, as are the pulpit decorated with miniatures and the 19th-century bishop's throne. On the last-mentioned is the representation of the original monastery held up by the figures of Moses and St Catherine, painted by an Armenian artist. All around on the walls are hung icons and paintings with scenes from the Old and New Testaments.

Suspended from the 18th-century wooden ceiling with

The famous mosaic of the Transfiguration.

A richly decorated panel.

A general view and a detail of two panels of the magnificent iconostasis in the Basilica.

Overall view of the iconostasis.

In this fresco dominated by the Virgin and Child, we can observe an ancient depiction of the monastery flanked by the figures of Moses and St Catherine.

gold stars on a green background are some fifty lamps and candelabra, most of which with ostrich eggs.

According to Orthodox tradition, the altar is located after the iconostasis. This is formed of four wooden panels, inlaid and gilded, with the icons of *Christ*, the *Blessed Virgin Mary, St Catherine* and *St John the Baptist*. Above, there is an impressive *Christ on the Cross*. The iconostasis was painted by Jeremiah of Crete at the beginning of the 17th century, and was donated to the monastery by Kosmos, Patriarch of the island of Crete.

Behind the iconostasis, above the high altar, we find perhaps the most precious treasure in the basilica: the grandiose *mosaic of the Transfiguration*.

Datable to the 6th century, in the delicate harmony of its colours it is one of the finest mosaics that have come down to us. Similar in style to the mosaic of St Sophia in Istanbul, it represents the transfigured Christ in the centre, the two prophets Moses and Elijah to the left, and at the feet of Christ the apostles Peter, James and John. Thirty other portraits follow:

The so-called "Moses' well", where the phophet is said to have encountered Jethro's daughters.

The place indicated by tradition as the one in which Moses supposedly saw the burning bush.

those of St John the Baptist, the Blessed Virgin, the Evangelists, prophets from the Old Testament, and the Apostles.

The figures were painted in blue, red and green on a dark- gold abstract background.

The high altar consists of a beautiful marble slab, encrusted with mother-of-pearl and supported by six slender columns: it is a fine work by an artist who was active in Athens during the 17th century.

The two sarcophaghi located there are the gift of two Russian tsars: Peter the Great, who donated one to the monastery in 1680, and Alexander II, in 1860. Here, as we have already said, are preserved the precious remains of the Saint, illuminated day and night by numerous silver oil-lamps.

CHAPEL OF THE BURNING BUSH

In this chapel, the most venerated of the entire monastery, the visitor enters even today without his shoes, just as Moses too did at God's command, in honour of the holiness of the place: "*...put off thy shoes from off thy feet, for the place where thou standest is holy ground*" (Exodus, 3:5).

Here, as tradition would have it, Moses saw the bush burning without being consumed; here, God manifested Himself to Moses for the first time in all His tremendous power. The chapel is very small, barely three by five metres, but it is richly decorated with a lovely blue ceramic. An altar supported by four slender marble columns rises on the spot in which it is said that the bush had its roots. This was then transplanted outside, in order to permit erection of the altar over the roots.

Even if, as a rule, they are not accessible to the large masses of tourists who arrive at the monastery, it is however possible — upon request — also to visit the other buildings that make up part of the monastery complex.

In a curious architectural and symbolic contrast, next to the Basilica is located the **Mosque**: very simple, rec-

tangular in shape, with a minaret about ten and a half
metres high. Today it serves not only for the pilgrims
of the Islamic faith who visit St Catherine, but also for
the Muslim personnel working at the monastery. Next
to the minaret rises the three-storey **bell tower**, built
during the 19th century by the monk Gregorius. The
nine bells in the tower, each one different, are a gift
from the Russian Church.

The other more important buildings in the monastery
are the refectory and the library. The **old refectory** is
entered from the basilica: it is a rectangular room, 17
metres long and 5 metres wide, illuminated by a single
corridor and covered with gothic arches. A wooden
table inlaid with sacred and floral motifs is outstand-
ing; on the walls, there is the usual beautiful display of
pictures and icons.

The boast of the St Catherine monastery is the **Library**,
15 metres long and more than 10 metres wide. In it are
preserved precious codices and manuscripts for which
the monastery is justly famous. For the number and
value of the volumes the St Catherine collection is second in importance only to the Vatican library. In it

are preserved more than 6,000 manuscripts and
volumes, most of them in Greek and the rest in more
than ten languages: among which Arabic, Armenian,
Coptic, Georgian, Syriac. The texts are mainly theo-
logical, but there are also historical and scientific
tomes. Among others, from this library come two of
the most important and well-known codices of ancient
times: the *Codex Syriacus* and the *Codex Sinaiticus*.
The former, discovered at the end of the 19th century,
is the version of the Gospels in Syriac and can be dated
to the 4th century.

The latter can also boast an adventurous history.
Together with the *Codex Alexandrinus* in London, the
Codex Vaticanus in Rome and the *Codex Ephraem* in
Paris, this codex, that was discovered in the
monastery, is among the most precious codices of the
Bible. It is the copy of the Greek original of the New
Testament. Its great value lies in the fact that up until
now it has been the only copy to come down to us of
the original in Greek of the New Testament. The text
was perhaps drawn up in Cesarea, and its discovery
turned all of the Biblical theories upside-down be-

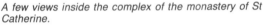
A few views inside the complex of the monastery of St Catherine.

cause, from a painstaking reading of it, it was discovered that St Mark's gospel was written before those of St Matthew and St Luke.

Until 24 February 1859, the Codex was jealously guarded by the monks in the monastery. Then, on that day a scholar from Leipzig, Konstantin von Tischendorf, arrived at the monastery with a letter authorizing him to take the codex and to remove it temporarily in order to make a copy of it. From that moment on the monks never saw it again. Taken to St Petersburg, it was given as a gift to Tsar Alexander II; then, following the Russian Revolution in 1917, the precious codex was sold for 100,000 pounds sterling in England, where it is still today preserved in the British Museum.

Together with the Codices the monastery also possesses the most important collection of icons in the world. There are more than 2,000 items, dating from the 5th to the 7th centuries, many of which are made with the encaustic technique. There are also numerous items dating from the iconoclastic period, when the monastery of St Catherine remained the only place in which sacred images managed to escape destruction.

The Chapel of St Triphone: the outside and inside with the skulls of the monks.

Beyond the walls, on the northwest side, the monastery's very green garden opens up with a magnificent panorama. Built on terracings and surrounded by cypress trees, many qualities of fruit trees grow there: oranges, lemons, olives, pears and apricots, not to mention grape vines.

The chapel which looms up next to the garden is that of St Triphone: in it is the *charnel house* for the monastery, which contains hundreds and thousands of skulls and bones of the monks who have lived, prayed and died there.

One skeleton is completely clothed, with a purple hat: it is St Stephen, who died there in 580.

An outside view of the monastery.

ST CATHERINE

The saint whose name is given to the monastery was born in Alexandria in the year 294, to a rich and noble family, and was named Dorothy. Converted and baptized as a Christian, she was tortured several times; but she never denied her faith, and was beheaded on 25 November 305. Legend has it that when she underwent her martyrdom, milk instead of blood came out of her wounds.

Buried in Alexandria, five centuries passed before a monk from Sinai had a vision of the Saint's body that was being transported by the angels to the summit of a nearby mountain where it would remain intact. When some monks went up on the mountain, they found the undecayed body of the virgin martyr, from which emanated a very sweet myhrr that was collected in ampoules because it was considered miraculous. There was then a monk named Simon who, it was said, remained for seven years next to the Saint's body, praying that she would give him a part of her hand. Finally, three fingers detached themselves from the Saint's left hand, and the monk took them to the Abbey of the Holy Trinity in Rouen.

All this news, narrated by the Crusaders on their return from the Holy Land, spread all over Europe, and Catherine — whose historicity has still been impossible to prove, even up until now — became one of the most popular saints in the Christian world. Finally, the monks decided to carry the relics from the mountain to the monastery, and both took on the Saint's name: the former, Gebel Kathrina (Katrin); the latter, Monastery of St Catherine.

All of this took place probably between the 10th and the 11th centuries. The skull of the Saint, bound by a crown of gold encrusted with precious stones, and the left hand with rings and gems, were enclosed in precious silver coffers and kept in a sarcophagus next to the altar of the Church of the Transfiguration.

Every November 25th, the anniversary of the martyrdom undergone by the Saint, a magnificent procession is held in the Church, with the two reliquaries being carried around the Basilica.

*Two wintertime views of Gebel Musa, or Moses'
Mountain.*

MOSES' MOUNTAIN (GEBEL MUSA)

Somewhat isolated, to the south of the monastery of
St Catherine, Gebel Musa (or Moses' mountain) rises
with its 2,285 metres: it is the one which tradition iden-
tifies with Mount Horeb in the Bible — here, the God
of Israel reportedly gave Moses the Tables of the Law
containing the Ten Commandments. Considered
sacred by the three monolithic religions (Hebrew,
Christian and Islam), Gebel Musa is reached after an
ascent of about three hours. Several paths lead to the
summit, the most well- known of which is the "sikket
Sayidna Musa", or path of our Lord Moses, which begins immediately after the monastery.
Halfway up, the pilgrim encounters a spring named
"Mayet Musa", or "Moses' water", where it is said
that the prophet watered his flock. The so-called
"Moses' stairway" is composed of three hundred

granite steps, which legend claims were arranged by a
single monk in order to fulfil a vow. We then arrive at
the "door of confessions", where pilgrims confessed
themselves to a hermit who always lived in the place.
Only after the absolution could the faithful continue
their climb towards the summit and reach the "door of
faith" where they left their shoes and, barefoot like
Moses before God, arrived at the top. Here, Justinian
had had a small chapel erected, which was destroyed
several times: over the ruins of the last chapel, in 1934
was built the church that we see at present.
The remains of the second edifice are those of a
mosque: this is the place in which, as the Bedouins say,
Naabi Saleh was supposedly taken up into heaven.
Most visitors prefer to await the dawn up there, when
the first rays of the sun illuminate all of the surrounding rocks and penetrate to the south until they light up
the Gulf of Aqaba.

61

Another view of Moses' Mountain: the chapel almost blends into the rocks.

One of the paths leading up to the sacred mountain.

An aerial view over the summit of Moses' Mountain.

The warm light of the sunset bestows a very special colour on the rocks of Sinai.

MOUNTAIN OF ST CATHERINE (GEBEL KATHRINA)

With its 2,642 metres this is the highest mountain of the entire Sinai peninsula. It owes its name to the fact that, as is handed down by legend, the angels reportedly transported here the body of the saint who had been martyred in Alexandria.

A walk of at least five hours is necessary in order to ascend to its peak. Along the way, the **Monastery of the 40 Martyrs (Deir al Arbain)** can be seen. It recalls the monks killed by the Blemmi tribe.

On the summit is located the **chapel** dedicated to St Catherine, built by the monk Callisto: a drapery in-

The white building surmounted by the cupola close to the Monastery of St Catherine is the tomb of Nabi Saleh, the prophet Saleh whom the Bedouins of Sinai have always venerated as their local saint.

Three views of the countryside surrounding St Catherine: a Bedouin with his camel and the rocks eroded by the wind.

On the following pages: four facets of the mountains around St Catherine.

dicates the place in which the body of St Catherine was reportedly found.

Two rooms are set up adjacent to the chapel in order to give refuge to the pilgrims and tourists who spend the night there.

When the day is clear, the view that can be enjoyed from the summit of Gebel Kathrina is incomparable: almost the entire Sinai peninsula is spread out like an enormous fan of stone and rocks, before our eyes, from the Gulf of Suez to the Gulf of Aqaba, as far as the African mountains to the west and the mountains of the Arab peninsula to the east.

Plants and Flowers: Life in the Desert

Despite the aridity of the soil and the inclement climate, the desert is at times surprising. An incredible number of types of vegetation succeed (and admirably) in surviving in near-prohibitive environmental conditions.
On these two pages, only a few of the species of flora that thrive in this microcosm.

Feiran, the "pearl of Sinai", with its beautifully green oasis abounding in palm trees and tamarisks.

OASIS OF FEIRAN

"And all the congregation of the children of Israel journeyed from the wilderness of Sin, after their journeying, according to the commandment of the Lord, and pitched in Rephidim....Then came Amalek and fought with Israel in Rephidim" (Exodus, 17:1,8). The biblical Rephidim is today's Feiran, the place which the Arabs like to define as the "pearl of Sinai": surrounded by gigantic rocky masses, dominated by Gebel Serbal, an altitude of 2078 metres, this oasis appears to us today like a genuine paradise. It extends for almost four kilometers, a very green strip of date palms and tamerisks, interrupted by the houses made of dried earth. A little of everything is cultivated there,

from corn to barley, from wheat to tamarisks; but the main harvest is still dates. Here, therefore, according to the Bible, Israel fought its first battle and, still in Exodus (17,11), it is recounted that "...*when Moses held up his hand,...Israel prevailed: and when he let down his hand, Amalek prevailed*".

On this traditional site of the battle, won in the end by the Israelites guided by Joshua, there subsequently arose a small monastery that is dependent on the Monastery of St Catherine.

Today, several interesting icons, stone capitals and trunks of columns going back to the 5th century, are

Several views of the Feiran oasis: the church, which still today remains inside the monastery, the small driveway up to the church, a view of the oasis and the ruins of the ancient church of Feiran.

The countryside constantly offers unexpected and curious sights: a cluster of palm trees, a solitary acacia, the dried-up bed of a stream, green in colour.

preserved in the monastery's tiny church. As for the city of Feiran, it appears to be mentioned already in the 2nd century, and it became the episcopal seat from the 4th century until the 7th century. Many monks and hermits came there to seek a refuge where they could pray and meditate, until they were driven out by the Muslims. The monastery fell into ruins, and a basilica and two churches disappeared that Feiran had had in the 12th century during a brief period of renaissance. Only some charming ruins remain today of these last-mentioned buildings, ruins which almost merge with the rock of the mountains.

A jeepful of tourists ventures along the road that leads towards the "Coloured Canyon".

A section of the canyon, characterized by very white calcareous rocks.

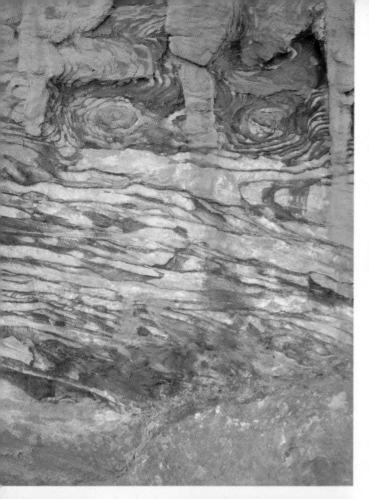

Nature has had fun modelling the rocks in the canyon, indulging her whims with the colours and shapes: the so-called "elephant's feet" are characteristic of this section.

On the following pages:
four views of the entry to the "Coloured Canyon".

About 100 km from Sharm el Sheikh is Dahab, a small center of
'informal' tourism that extends through high mountains and three
oases overlooking the Gulf of Aqaba. The tourist will find no large
hotel complexes here, but rather the natural beauty spots
illustrated on these pages and the cordial atmosphere for which
this locality is known.

Nuweiba, a town north of Dahab,
is becoming a preferred vacation spot.
With its beautiful beaches, splendid
coastal reef, and residential complexes.
In the photographs, views of the beaches
and characteristic corners of the town.

The stretch of coast
north of Nuweiba toward Taba,
located near the Israeli border.

Pharaoh's Island, a few
kilometers before Taba. On the island,
surrounded by magnificent coral reefs, is
an ancient fortress visited by many tourists.

The Underwater World

A submersion into the depths of the barrier reef of the Red Sea is a unique occasion for coming close to an untouched, fairyland-like Nature.

Contrary to what is commonly believed, underwater fishing is a sport that everyone can practice: you not have to possess special physical attributes. Every morning, scores of boats loaded with tourists leave the landing stages of Sharm el Sheikh and head for the places where the most beautiful depths and most interesting coral formations can be admired. You do not have to be an expert underwater fisherman to be able to admire it all: all you need is a mask, a few swimming strokes away from the shore, and you are immersed in an unreal world where space and sound no longer make sense.

The Emperor Angelfish (Pomacanthus imperator), *as a juvenile (above) and adult.*

What is so astounding, apart from the thousands of species of tropical fish present there, are the infinite varieties of coral. And it is also curious to think that only in the 18th century did man realize that corals are not marine vegetation, but rather the calcareous skeletons of anthozoans. Fortunately, these corals cannot be taken away; so, as long as man continues to protect this oasis of peace and natural beauty, they will continue to wave magically and to populate this unreal underwater world.

*On the facing page, a manta ray (*Manta sp.*) and a school of barracuda (*Sphyraena sp.*).*

*On this page, a Circular Batfish (*Platax orbicularis*) and a Bluefin Trevally (*Caranx melampygus*).*

*On the following pages, a group of Sabre Squirrelfish (*Adioryx spinifer*) and a Lionfish (*Pterois volitans*).*

Two Coral Groupers
(Cephalopholis miniata).

*A Peacock Rock Cod
(*Cephalopholis argo*)
and a Greasy Grouper
(*Epinephelus tauvina*).*

*On the following pages,
various examples of frogfish
(*Antennarius sp.*).*

*A Common Sea Turtle
(Caretta caretta) and an
Imbricated Turtle
(Eretmochelys imbricata).*

Another Imbricated Turtle
(Eretmochelys imbricata)
and a Green Turtle
(Chelonia mydas).

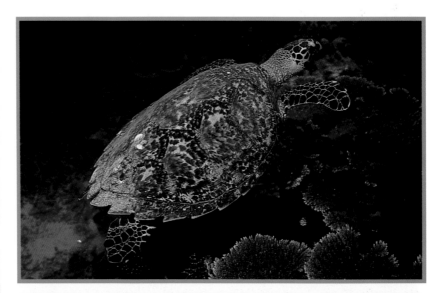

An example of the "nude" mollusc of the genus Chromodoris *and a* Dendrophyllia *coral.*

On the facing page, another of the "nude" molluscs of the genus Phyllidia *and a* mushroom- like Fungia *coral.*

On the following pages, a splendid Gorgonian sea fan (Melithaea sp.).

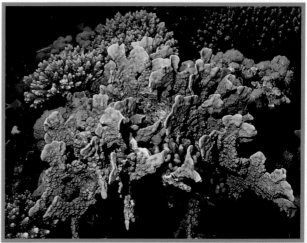

On the facing page, top left and bottom, the White Stingng Sea Fan (Lytocarpus philippinus); top right, a Slab Fire Coral (Millepora platyphylla).

Top left, a Leucetta chagosensis sponge; top right, the Stylasterid Coral (Distichopora violacea); bottom right, Distichopora sp.

A female or juvenile Axilspot Hogfish (Bodianus axillaris) and a male Tricolor Parrotfish (Scarus tricolor).

Above, three Common Lizardfish (Synodus variegatus) and a spectacular Orange- striped Triggerfish (Balistapus undulatus).
Center, a Blue Triggerfish (Pseudobalistes fuscus) and a black Redtooth Triggerfish (Odonus niger).
Bottom, a Humbug Damselfish (Dascyllus aruanus) and a juvenile Domino (Dascyllus trimaculatus) with its characteristic white spots.

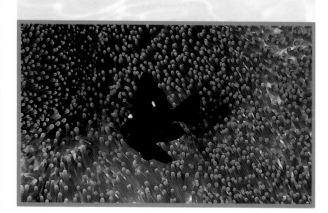

109

A Blacktip Grouper (Epinephelus fasciatus), a Half-and-Half Chromis (Chromis dimidiata), and a bright Yellowsaddle Goatfish (Parupeneus cyclostomus).

On the facing page, three Blotcheye Soldierfish (Myripristus murdjan) and a Diana's Hogfish (Bodianus diana).

On the preceding pages, a school of Yellowfin Goatfish (Mulloides vanicolensis).

On this page, various species of Sarcophyton *(soft corals)* and *(right center)* a True Oyster *(*Lopha cristagalli*).*

Top right, another member of the genus Sarcophyton; *bottom right, an* Alcyonacea (Scleronephtya corymbosa). *Left, another soft coral and two* Alcyonaceae (Dendronephtya sp.).

On the facing page, a juvenile (top) and an adult Cube Trunkfish (Ostracion cubicus).

On this page, a well-protected Porcupinefish (Diodon hystrix) and a Giant Clam (Tridacna maxima), which adopts a completely different defensive strategy.

Dangerous Animals

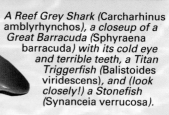

A Reef Grey Shark *(Carcharhinus amblyrhynchos), a closeup of a Great Barracuda (Sphyraena barracuda) with its cold eye and terrible teeth, a Titan Triggerfish (Balistoides viridescens), and (look closely!) a Stonefish (Synanceia verrucosa).*

An elegant Sailfin Surgeonfish
(Zebrasoma desjardinii) and a Black
Stingray (Taeniura melanospilos).

A Giant Moray (Gymnothorax javanicus), a brittle star (Ophiotrix sp.), and an Electric ray (Torpedo sinuspersici).

On the facing page, Moon Jellyfish (Aurelia aurita) and Net Fire Coral (Millepora dichotoma).

Some recipes of the Red Sea Cuisine

Falafel or Ta'amia
Fava bean croquettes

250 g/ 8 oz Dried fava beans	Cumin
1 Onion	Parsley
Flour	Green salad, for garnish
Baking powder	Tahin
1 Clove garlic	Olive oil

Clean the beans by removing the thin skin and soak in water for 5-6 hours. Put them in the blender along with the sliced onion, 1 sprig parsley, the garlic, a teaspoon of cumin and a pinch of baking powder.
Place the mixture into a bowl and thicken with a couple of tablespoons flour if necessary. Shape into walnut sized balls and set aside for 20 minutes. Coat with flour and fry in hot oil until golden. Drain on paper towels. Place on a tray and serve hot with *tahin* and green salad.

Ful Mudammas
Fava bean salad

250 g/ 8 oz Dried fava beans	2 Hard boiled eggs
2 Cloves garlic	2 Green onions
Cumin	1 Lemon
Parsley	Olive oil

Soak the beans for 5-6 hours; drain and put into a pot filled with cold water. Gradually bring to the boil and then simmer for about 2 and 1/2 hours. Drain. In a salad bowl combine the beans with the crushed garlic, salt and lemon juice.
Set aside for 15 minutes and serve lukewarm with onion rings, chopped parsley, cumin, pepper, olive oil and sliced hardboiled eggs on the side so that each guest can choose his or her condiments.

Khubz Ruqaq
Fenugreek bread

450 g/ 1 lb. Flour *Fenugreek (seeds)*

Sift the flour together with 1 tablespoon salt, and mound it on your work table: add 1 teaspoon of fenugreek seeds and a drop of water. Knead the dough, adding water as you go along, to obtain an elastic dough; this should take about 15 minutes. Dust the dough with flour, cover with a dry cloth and set aside for about 30 minutes. Divide the dough into 10-12 equal size pieces and shape them into very thin disks. Dust each disk with flour and fold in half; place them on a dry cloth and cover with another cloth; set aside for 30 minutes. Open the disks and place them on an oven pan; bake at 220 °C/ 425 °F for 8-10 minutes.

Kawareh bi Hummus
Trotter soup

1 Calf's trotter	*Ground turmeric*
200 g/ 8 oz Dried	*2 eggs*
chick peas	*Olive oil*

Soak the chick peas for five-six hours. Rinse the trotter and scald it in boiling water for 15 minutes; drain and dry. Brown the trotter in a pan with 4 tablespoons olive oil, a dash of salt and pepper and a teaspoon of turmeric. Add the drained chick peas and cover with water. When it boils lower the flame and simmer slowly for about 3 hours. Remove the trotter from the broth, bone and cut the meat into strips; put the meat back into the pan with the chick peas and reheat. In the meantime, hard boil the eggs (about 7 minutes), shell and chop. Sprinkle the chopped egg over the hot soup and serve.

Khabli Palau
Lamb with apricots

600 g/ 1¹/₂ lbs. Lean lamb	*Raisins*
400 g/ 14 oz Long grain rice	*Cinnamon and nutmeg*
150 g/ 6 oz Dried apricots	*Saffron (one packet)*
1 Onion	*100 g/ 4 oz Butter*

Have the butcher cut the meat into bite-size chunks; sprinkle with 1 teaspoon of ground cinnamon, salt and pepper, saffron and nutmeg. Chop the onion and sauté in a pan with 50 g/ 2 oz melted butter; add the meat.
Add ¹/₂ liter (2 cups) boiling, salted water, cover and cook slowly for 30 minutes. Add the apricots, 1 tablespoon raisins, cover and cook for another 30 minutes.
Cook the rice and drain before it is completely done. Grease an oven dish with butter and put half the rice into it. Put the meat and fruits over the rice, cover with another layer of rice. Cover the dish with a sheet of aluminum foil at bake at 160 °C/ 325 °F for 30 minutes.

Lissan al Assfour
Stewed lamb with egg barley

700 g/ 1 ¹/₂ lbs.	Cinnamon
Lean boned lamb	Aged pecorino cheese
250 g/ 8 oz Egg barley	Olive oil
2 Onions	Vegetable broth

Clean the onions, slice thinly and sauté gently in a skillet with four tablespoons olive oil; cut the meat into bite-size chunks and brown it with the onions. Add a dash each of salt and pepper, and one teaspoon ground cinnamon, cover and cook slowly for 15 minutes. Moisten with 2 glasses of hot broth and continue cooking covered over a moderate flame for 1 hour. Add 2 more ladles of broth, when it reaches the boil again, add the egg barley. As soon as it is cooked (about 7-8 minutes) serve the exquisite lissan al assfour with grated pecorino cheese.

Samak bi Tahina
Fish with sesame paste

1,2 kg/ 2 ¹/₂ lbs. Sea bream
or dentrix (2 whole fish)
2 Onions
2 Cloves garlic
Tahin
1 Lemon
Olive oil

Gut, wash, skin and filet the fish. Clean the onions, and chop together finely with the garlic; sauté in a skillet with 3-4 tablespoons olive oil. Remove the skillet from the stove, let cook and blend in 3 tablespoons *tahin,* the lemon juice, a little water and salt and pepper. Spread this mixture over the fish, salt lightly and place them in a greased oven dish. Cover with a sheet of aluminum foil and bake at 180 °C/ 350 °F for 20 minutes. Remove the foil and brown 10 minutes longer.

Samak Kebab
Fish kebabs

1,2 kg/ 2 ¹/₂ lbs. Bass
(or other white
Mediterranean fish)
4 Ripe tomatoes
2 Lemons
(plus one for garnish)

2 Onions
Cumin
Bay leaves
Parsley
Olive oil

Combine 12 tablespoons olive oil and the juice of 1 lemon in a bowl, add a pinch of salt and pepper, and 1 tablespoon cumin. Gut, wash, skin and filet the fish; cut it into bite-size pieces and marinate in the oil and lemon emulsion for 30 minutes. Prepare the skewers, alternating a piece of fish, tomato slice, bay leaf, lemon slice and onion. Cook over a charcoal grill or under the broiler for about 20 minutes, baste often with the marinade. Serve hot garnished with parsley, bay leaves and lemon slices.

Kamouneya
Stew with cumin

600 g/ 1¹/₂ lbs. Lean beef
4 Cloves garlic
Vegetable broth
Cumin

Parsley
150 g/ 6 oz
Boiled rice
Olive oil

Cut the meat into stew-sized chunks and brown evenly in a pan with 4 tablespoons olive oil; add the peeled, chopped garlic, a pinch of salt and one tablespoon cumin. When the meat is golden brown, add two ladles of vegetable broth, cover and cook slowly for 45 minutes, until the meat is tender enough to break with a fork. Serve this wonderful stew piping hot over boiled rice with a bit of chopped parsley.

Shish Kebab
Kebabs with saffron

700 g/ 1¹/₂ lbs. Lean beef
Saffron (1 packet)
2 Lemons
2 Onions
100 g/ 4 oz Parsley

Prepare the marinade by combining the chopped onion, salt, pepper, the saffron and the juice of 1 lemon. Cut the meat into 5 cm (2 inch) cubes and marinate it for 5-6 hours. Drain and arrange the meat on four skewers, cook on the grill or under the broiler for about 3 minutes on each of the four exposed sides. Finely chop the parsley and distribute it on a serving platter. When the meat is done, place the skewers on a bed of parsley and serve immediately garnished with thin lemon slices.

Michoteta
Cheese salad

350 g/ 13 oz Cream cheese
(or very thick yogurt)
1 Onion
1 Cucumber
2 Lemons
Olive oil

In a bowl, soften the cheese with a fork until it is very creamy; dress it with the lemon juice combined with 6-8 tablespoons olive oil, set aside for 30 minute. Clean the onion and chop it finely, cut the cucumber into cubes and mix them into the cheese, season with salt and pepper and stir gently. This salad too, served with one of the breads makes a full meal, or it is a wonderful side dish when served with fish such as Samak Kebab.

Malfuf Mahshi
Stuffed cabbage

1 Cabbage
500 g/ 1 lb. Lean chopped beef or lamb
100 g/ 4 oz Rice
1 Onion
2 Lemons
Dried mint
Ground cinnamon
Paprika

Wash the cabbage, separate the leaves and scald them in slightly salted boiling water for 4 minutes. Drain and remove the hard rib. Rinse the rice and combine it in a bowl with the meat, the finely chopped onion, and a dash each of salt, pepper, cinnamon and paprika. Place the meat mixture on the cabbage leaves, roll them into little bundles. Use the remaining leaves to line a pan, arrange the stuffed cabbage rolls on top; cover with water and simmer for 45 minutes; add 1 teaspoon crushed dried mint leaves and the juice of the lemons and cook for another 10 minutes. Serve immediately.

Balila
Barley pudding

300 g/ 12 oz Pearl barley
Shelled almonds and pistachio nuts

For the syrup:
150 g/ 6 oz Sugar
1 Lemon
Orange flower oil

Soak the barley in water for 3-4 hours. Boil it for about 1 hour until tender, then drain and put it into a bowl. Dissolve the sugar in 2 glasses of water and the juice of $^1/_2$ lemon; simmer until the syrup thickens; add 2 tablespoons orange flower oil. Pour the syrup over the barley: let cool, then arrange it on a tray and sprinkle chopped almonds and pistachios on top.

Contents